Zeffry Alkatiri

Zeffry Alkatiri

From Batavia to Jakarta in Poetry

English Translations by Deborah Cole
German translations by Michael Groß

BTW

LONTAR

Zeffry Alkatiri
From Batavia to Jakarta in Poetry
(a trilingual edition in English, German, and Indonesian)
All poems in this book were taken from
Dari Batavia Sampai Jakarta 1619-1999:
Peristiwa Sejarah Dan Kebudayaan Betawi-Jakarta Dalam Sajak
first published by Indonesiatera of Magelang in 2001.

Jl. Danau Laut Tawar No. 53, Jakarta 10210 Indonesia
www.lontar.org

BTW is an imprint of the Lontar Foundation

Editorial Team:
John H McGlynn (Senior Editor)
Yusi Avianto Pareanom (Indonesian-language Managing Editor)
Nirwan Dewanto & Nukila Amal (Co-editors)
Pamela Allen (English-language Managing Editor)
Jan Budweg (German-language Managing Editor)
Saira Kasim & Wikan Satriati (Editorial Assistants)

Publication of this book was made possible, in part,
with the generous assistance of BNI 46

Partial funding for its translation was provided by
the Translation Funding Program of Badan Pengembangan
dan Pembinaan Bahasa,
the Ministry of Education and Culture, the Republic of Indonesia.

Design and layout by Emir Hakim Design
Printed in Indonesia by PT Suburmitra Grafistama
ISBN No. 978-602-6978-01-1

Contents

1619-1942

1943-1965

1966-1999

by the way…

(a note from the publisher)

Since its establishment in 1987, the Lontar Foundation of Jakarta, a non-profit organization devoted to the promotion of Indonesian literature, has focused on the goal of creating a canon of Indonesian literature in English translation. With that as its mission, the Foundation has published close to 200 books containing translations of literary work by several hundred Indonesian authors. In its 28 years of existence, Lontar has published numerous significant and landmark works. By the end of this year, 2015, for instance, Lontar's Modern Library of Indonesia series will contain fifty titles by many of Indonesia's most important authors, with representative literary work spanning the entire twentieth century and beyond. These titles, together with *The Lontar Anthology of Indonesian Drama*, *The Lontar Anthology of Indonesian Short Stories*, and *The Lontar Anthology of Indonesian Poetry*–the latter two of which will be published this year–will make it possible to teach and foster appreciation of Indonesian literature anywhere in the world through the medium of English. Further, with changes in print technology, Lontar's titles are now available throughout the world in a matter of days and for a fraction of the cost in former times.

The authors whose work Lontar has published are recognized by both foreign and Indonesian literary critics and literati as some of the best writers Indonesia has ever produced. Naturally, however, given the scope of time covered by Lontar publications (from the late nineteenth century to the present) many of these authors are now elderly or already deceased. Which is why Lontar has now developed a new imprint, BTW Books, through which the Foundation will now begin to introduce to the world other talented Indonesian writers whose work is hardly known outside the country's borders yet has been deemed by both literary critics and Lontar's editorial board to be worthy of international attention. (In general, authors who already have one or more books available in translation, either in English or another major international language, were not considered for inclusion in this, the first stage of the series.)

Because of the abundance of talented Indonesian authors, the selection of the first 25 authors was difficult to make, but Lontar's hope is that if the series proves successful in achieving its goal, the Foundation will then be able to produce translations by another 25 authors and then another 25 authors and so on in the years to come.

Because of the not-for-profit nature of Lontar's work, none of Lontar's numerous ventures would be possible without the generosity of others. In the case of BTW Books, Lontar is especially grateful to BNI 46 for its generosity in underwriting a large percentage of the cost of this series' publication. Lontar is also grateful to the authors in this first stage of the series who, in their knowledge of the promotional nature of this series, agreed to forego royalties and other forms of monetary recompense. Lontar must also thank Emir Hakim and his design team; the many talented translators who contributed much valuable time to this project; and, last but not least, my editorial board and staff who selflessly devoted themselves to the goal of making this project a success.

John H McGlynn

Introducing Zeffry J Alkatiri

Zeffry J Alkatiri was born in Jakarta in 1960. He is an instructor and researcher in the Department of History in the Faculty of Humanities at the University of Indonesia. He is also an author and a poet. His books of poetry have several times been awarded first prize from the Jakarta Arts Council (Dewan Kesenian Jakarta) (2000), the Ikapi Main Book Foundation (Yayasan Buku Utama Ikapi) (2002), and the Equator Literary Award (Khatulistiwa Literary Award) (2012). He has participated in several international literature programs: like the Winternachten Literature Festival (2000, 2002 dan 2008), the International Literary Festival (2001), and the Ubud Writer Reader Festival (2009). His published volumes of poetry include *Dari Batavia Sampai Jakarta 1619-1999: Peristiwa Sejarah Dan Kebudayaan Betawi-Jakarta Dalam Sajak [From Batavia to Jakarta 1619-1999: Historical Events and the Culture of Betawi-Jakarta in Poetry,* 2000], *When Will You Came Back Jaap?* (2002), *Catatan Perjalanan Seorang Hadrami [Travel Notes of a Hadrami,* 2004], *Post*

Kolonial dan Wisata Sejarah dalam Sajak [Post Colonial and Travel History in Verse, 2012], and *My Allah, My Apostle, and Your Hajj* (2014). Several of his poems have been translated into English, Portuguese, Dutch, Russian and Chinese.

E

The Seal of the City of Batavia: May 30, 1619

Palm wine and
Chinese arak
tickle the throats
and warm the veins
of the sojourners
at Sunda Calapa port.

The leftover bitter vinegary vapor
assaults the visage of the lion Major
who hails from the city of Hoorn.
Hungrily,
he settles
                lurks
                calculates
                ensnares

and preys with his
victims in his tapering fingers.

Every day, inch by inch
cubit by cubit

confidently
the lanky Major
covers and conjures the Jacatra swamp
converting it to Kastil Batavia.

Coyly
he seduces crew, soldiers, and slaves
into feeling his pointed fangs:
sharp as spears.
Their blood splatters
over the tower walls of Fort Mauritius and Fort
Nassau.
Congealed drops
become an offering that the Major sends
to the Batavier ancestors
in Hollandia.

Amsterdam–Batavia

Nutmeg, pepper, and cloves
sting the ears and clog up the noses
of the Dutch merchants and sailors.
Maluku and Banda's island winds
broadcast the delivery of spice shipments into
distant underground cellars.

Amsterdam and Batavia are busy preparing
maps, ships' holds, and warehouses.
The crew in the stern inhales the scent
of sweet-smelling, fragrant spices
as the ocean spray scatters sparkles of gold
into their eyes.

Anchors are thrown, cannons ignited.
Balls of fire echo in Ternate,
Tidore, Banda, and Ambone.
The bellies of ships are loaded full.
Forests are demolished as trees are uprooted.
Spices are melted and fused to become
church walls and belfries

prisons
town halls
highways
palaces
and Club Concordia.

A portion is pawned for supplies of
                    ammunition
                    cheese
                    bread
                    books
                    lamps
                    brandy
                    maidens and mistresses.

What's left is taken to a heavenly keep
where *gloria* is written on every door.
While Captain Jas stands waiting
in the Kebon Jahe Kober cemetery,
Hermes, Mars, Apollo, Cupid, the angels, Christ,
        and Mary
stand watch over the sailors every night as they sleep.

Awaiting their grandchildren's return
from Batavia,

Omas and Opas
in Amsterdam
chatter and crochet, smoke pipes and drink tea,
while drunken skippers in beachside taverns
weep for their friends
who choked and died in the miry mud
of Batavia.

Valckenier: 1740

Like Nero,
he sits on the veranda
playing his lyre
allowing the fire to
dance on the Chinese settlements.

The Myth of the Foreign Orientals and the Natives

Admission to Gambir Fair: 1925

Op Gewone Dagen (Ordinary Days)	*Volwassenen* (Adults)	*Kinderen* (Children)
Europeanen (Europeans)	*f. 0.50*	*f. 0.25*
Vreemde Oosterlingen (Foreign Orientals)	*f. 0.25*	*f. 0.15*
Inlander (Natives)	*f. 0.15*	*f. 0.10*

East is East
and West is distant and disparate
and always delimited by
walls of

Uncertainty
Enmity
Dishonesty
Anxiety
Poverty
Ferocity
Savagery

Brutality

Stupidity

Discontinuity

Obscurity

Impenetrability

Obscenity

Duplicity

Apathy

Voracity

Tyranny

_____y…

Post Card: January 5, 1943

A *post kaart* in black and white
picturing the Paradeplaats.
Somber.
Displaying the lion monument.
Furious.
With JP Coen scolding vaguely
from the Wit Huis's back yard.

Beneath a 10-cent stamp
featuring a Nippon soldier
bearing the notification
Postal Savings Bank
is written the inscription:

My Dear Mother,
Happy New Year!

This would perhaps be his last
given that the Hermes on Harmoni Bridge's
feet are chained,
his eyes are closed and
his wings are clipped

Farewell!

Your son,

Hans E Van den Broecke.

Noordwijk–Pav 12 B

Batavia–Djakarta.

Entering the City: 1949

As told by an eyewitness

Already we've made ready
since yesterday
the flowers, flags, and banners
for the young fighters
from Kerawang and Tanggerang.

Maybe in the convoy there's still a
Jono, Suratman, Bachtiar, or an Idrus
our brothers, friends, and neighbors
who are now longhaired, filthy, and shabby
but who were once so stylish and dapper.
Everything was mortgaged the day Nica came to
town.

Already we've made ready
since yesterday
the songs that won't get heard and
the badges that won't be pinned.
It's all pointless
because the men are in a hurry to run off

to Menteng, Matraman, and Tanah Abang
in search of lodging, diversions, goods, and women.

We cheer for just a moment at Kramat
looking for faces we can no longer recognize.
Drifting like litter,
the throngs head silently home
carrying their wilting flowers
to be thrown away.

Mister Hendrik and His Son Jopie

Full-blooded-Dutch Mister Hendrik walked upright,
as upright as the silhouetted figures
on his bottles of drink.
From time to time he took his motorbike
the BSA built in nineteen fifty-five.

Young Master Jopie was his only child,
the product of a contract marriage
with a widowed Sundanese.
Jopie grew up to become a seasoned player,
and also an habitual tease.

Lucky for Mister Hendrik he wasn't a Nica veteran
so he could live easy in a Javanese village.
Mister Hendrik had worked for years at Nirom,
but upon retirement he took up duties at Philips-
Ralin.

Young Jopie was graduated from Van Lith-
Gunung Sahari High School,
and fortunately he could still *Holland Spreken*.

He landed a job as a Rathkamp pharmacist
but ended up as a broker at Unilever.

The invective voices of these two men
became their neighbors' breakfast fare.
In their living room hung a large poster
of the Rotterdamsche Lloyd
that never transported them anywhere.

Mister Hendrik was friendly, but often flustered.
Jopie was a troublemaker, gallant and cavalier.
They spent their salaries on prostitutes
who worked the corners in Kali Got and Gang
Hauber.
and who hailed from Krawang, Kuningan, and
Indramayu.

Sometimes, once every three months or so,
Mister Hendrik would head up to Cisarua
along with some of his Indo-Menado buddies
who liked playing cards.
While he was away, Jopie would steal
the keys to his father's *Motorfiets*
and run around the streets of Jakarta.

The rains come–Goats get going
The Dutch get drunk–Three days rolling
Puppets play–Until the morning
Japan gets drunk–The Dutch get going

Mister Hendrik and Jopie, his son
forgot the way to church
forgot to celebrate Christmas
and forgot their very own birthdays.
Mister Hendrik and Jopie, his son
are the vestigal grandchildren
of the company troops,
displaced and abandoned.
Mister Hendrik died all of a sudden.
Jopie died in a hit and run.
Both were thrown away like garbage
at Velbak.

The Beloved Missionary (Habib)

1

Welcome!
There's heavy, raspy coughing
everywhere in the Arab district.
High fences
and doors are all shut tight throughout the afternoon.
Women peek out carefully
verifying each and every visitor.
From behind grated windows
their rounded eyes
swoop down on their targets.
Their noses like hilly slopes
inhale the dust of death.
While Batavian bacteria diligently scrape away at
their throats.

2

Ahlan!
A sound from a dry pharyngeal cave
the missionary in his sarong
seated in a rattan chair
a steaming cup of ginger brew

rests on an octagonal marble table.
Prayer beads rotate in and around the fingers of
his left hand.
His right hand supports his turbaned head and
a clotting cloud hangs over him:

3

He was twenty-one years old
when last he saw the desert wadis.
He vomited on the deck of an English ship
from Aden to Betawi.
He was greeted with a verdant vision
when he finally set foot on fertile ground
ready to be sown with the law and the Hadith
rooted in his every brain cell.

4

Man, where ya goin, man?
I'm going to Pekojan.
Man, whadda sellin', man?
I'm selling beads of coral.

Habib bore herbal remedies to the Bandan
neighborhoods
he carried the word to the sanctuaries

he spread frankincense in homes and madrasahs.
Once every ten years he threw off his robes
and headed to Mecca to fling pebbles at the devil...
For forty-six years
the seeds he planted
spread to Batavia's distant corners.
And now Habib is homesick and wants to go home!

5

All along the Arab settlement
there's a call and response of hacking and
wheezing.
There's no chance of hiding from the bill collectors
while the Batavian bacteria persist in their plague
of wrecking throats and lungs.

After *Asr* prayers
doors begin to open.
Arabs are resting on platforms
and reclining on bamboo pallets
while sipping on their hookahs.

Ahlan... Bib!
His brew has turned cold.
The Maghrib drum sounds

his fingers stop moving
his prayer beads fall to the ground
his hand reaches down
and touches a floor
bereft of sand....

Batavia Centrum

1933:
Chinese women, young and old
Totter beneath
Buckets of sweat
Treading narrow lanes
between shops in Pintoe Ketjil

1942:
The Japanese arrive
Stupid bastard, they say
To the Chinese man in calico
Miserable from having
His godown plundered
No New Years this year
Moon cakes stuffed with coconut pulp

1954:
Chinese girls and boys
Unlatch their doors
And wait for coins
To fill donation baskets

1963:
Chinese men and women
Prop open their doors
To let the smoke of incense
Waft into their homes
Quietly, they tally
Bad days on an abacus

1979:
Tapeikong cooks are envious
To see the god of gambling
Offered incense every day
The Tans and Lies control the *chiefen*
Some of them visit the temple
Others kneel before Mother Mary

1992:
Elderly Chinese women and men
Walk unsteadily hand in hand
To the square for *tai-chi*
While their grandchildren in Singapore
Remain sound asleep

1998:
As the iron curtain crumbles

Jade statues of the goddess Kwan Im
And the tiger Pa Kua shatter
And are scattered with ancestors' ashes

Passage of Time: The Tanjung Priok Train Station

The late afternoon sun sticks out its tongue
straight across the intersection
and through the glass windows
of the fifty-foot tall Art-Deco building.

Twenty-six steel pole columns
curving in a half circle
shake hands at the apex
to form a giant mouth
ready to swallow humans and trains.

The bulging building births two more.
Its arms sturdily grip the ground.
Marble above and below,
its inner walls are decorated with little reliefs
in the styles of Italy and Java.
From outside
the structure looks like a primordial beast
which only time
can turn to dust.

In the waiting room
stylish young girls
chatter like a family of shrews
fighting over breadcrumbs.
Young *Maneers* wearing hats and Gatsby suits
stand hands on hips
waiting for the coach to arrive,
dandling their long-handled umbrellas
like characters in a silent film.

Several grandfathers sit cross-legged
studying the *Java Bode* newspaper,
while grandmothers in the VIP lounge
banter about a performance
by Tonniel Miss Riboet,
whose playbill remains plastered on the wall.

Sailors newly arrived from Singapore
are beckoned by the occasional "all aboard"
from the nearby docks.
Members of The Royal Netherlands
East India Army
on leave from their assignment in Aceh
stand alone
rolling fragrant Van Nelle tobacco.

The station master comes out of his guard post.
He looks up to check
the accuracy of his wristwatch,
and briefly talks with the platform clerks.
Across the tracks,
the porters are crouched awaiting orders.
The atmosphere is quiet
as in anticipation of the arrival of a corpse.

Everyone is suddenly
surprised by the appearance
of a group of adolescent boys
from Zandvoort, who enter, joking around
wearing beach hats and khaki shorts,
their sweat smelling like stale coconut milk.

Ah…!
I thought I was in the olden days,
but it turns out I'm foundering
in the Tanjung Priok train station.
The late afternoon sun grows fierce.
Its goggling eye stares at the station's giant mouth
that yearns to clamp its jaw shut,
its steel frame weary
of supporting the burden of bygone eras.

The columnar handshake blisters, threatening to
    come undone.

From outside
the building looks like a neglected dinosaur,
which only time
can turn to dust.

In the waiting room
the railway company staff practices volleyball,
their voices echoing excitement.
In the former VIP waiting room
some men play badminton
in a space partitioned like termites nests
into offices and storage.
In the yard outside
people lie around haphazardly
like refugees during the revolutionary war.
In every corner
dregs of urine seep and spread.
The place smells like it has been used to sell
    sacrificial animals.

From inside its belly
we ask ourselves,

Is there anything left for it to devour?
The Tanjung Priok Train Station
is a colossal cocoon
decomposing its own demise.

Seggelum Urbis Bataviae: 30. Mai 1619

Palmwein Palmsaft
Chinesischer Reisschnaps
Kitzeln die Kehlen
Und erhitzen die Blutadern
Derer die sich im Hafen
Sunda Calapa aufhalten.

Der Rest des scharfen essigsauren Dampfes
Schlägt ans Gesicht des Majors Löwe
Von der Stadt Hoorn.
Wie ein hungriger Löwe
Setzt er sich fest
        Späht
        Zählt
        Täuscht
Und macht die Opfer zur Beute
In seinen leicht nach hinten gebogenen Fingern.

Jeden Tag, Zentimeter für Zentimeter
Elle für Elle
Mit Entschlossenheit

Trocknet der hochgewachsene Major
Den Sumpf *Jacatra* aus und verwandelt ihn
Ins *Kastil Batavia.*

Wie ein verschämter Löwe
Überredet er die Vorbeikommenden, Soldaten und
Sklaven
Seine scharfen Eckzähne
So spitz wie ein Speer zu spüren.
Ihr Blut spritzt an die
Turmmauern der Festungen *Mauritius* und *Nassau.*
Einen Teil des geronnenen Bluts
Verschickt der Major und lässt es
Den Vorfahren der *Batavier*
In Holland überbringen.

Amsterdam – Batavia

Nelken, Muskatnüsse und Pfeffer
Stacheln verstopfen Nasen und Ohren
Der holländischen Seeleute und Kaufleute.
Der Wind von der Inselwelt der Molukken und
Bandas
Verbreitet die Nachricht dass die angesammelten
Gewürze schon die Kellerräume anfüllen.

Amsterdam – Batavia bereitet geschäftig
Schiffsräume, Lager und Karten vor.
Die Mannschaft am Heck schnuppert und riecht
Den Duft der Gewürze
Und das Meer lässt einen goldenen Glanz
In ihren Augen funkeln.

Anker werden geworfen, Kanonen abgeschossen
Feuerbälle hallen wider in Tidore,
Ternate, Banda und Ambone.
Sie stopfen die Schiffsbäuche voll
Und reißen die Bäume mitsamt den Wurzeln aus
Die zu flüssigen Geldern gemachten Gewürze

werden:
Mauern und Kirchtürme
Gefängnis
Rathaus
Hauptstraße
Palast
Und *Club Concordia.*

Ein Teil wird verpfändet um Vorräte anzulegen:
Munition
Käse
Brot
Bücher
Lampen
Brandy
Junge Mädchen und Konkubinen

Der Rest wird ins Gotteshaus gebracht
An jede Tür dort ist *Gloria* geschrieben.
In *Kebon Jahe, Kober*
Wartet *Kapten Jas* auf
Hermes, Mars, Apollo, Cupido, kleine Engel, *Maria*
Und *Christus*
Er begrüßt sie und leistet beim Schlafen jeden Tag
Gesellschaft.

Inzwischen warten sie auf die Rückkehr ihrer
Kinder und Enkel
Aus Batavia.
In Amsterdam
Häkeln Omas und schwatzen
Opas rauchen Pfeife und trinken Tee
Unterdessen beweinen in einigen Kneipen am
Strand
Kapitäne die Trinker sind ihre Gefährten
Die erstickten im glitschigen Schlamm

Batavias.

Valckenier: 1740

Wie Nero
Sitzt er auf der Veranda
Spielt dabei die Leier
Und lässt Feuerzungen
In der Kampungsiedlung der Chinesen tanzen.

Der Mythos *Vreemde Oosterlingen* und *Inlander*

Eintrittspreise Pasar Gambir: 1925

Op Gewone Dagen	*Volwassenen*	*Kinderen*
Europeanen	*f. 0.50*	*f. 0.25*
Vreemde Oosterlingen	*f. 0.25*	*f. 0.15*
Inlander	*f. 0.15*	*f. 0.10*

Osten ist Osten
Weit entfernt und verschieden vom Westen
Immer abgegrenzt durch
Mauern:

Anrüchigkeit
Bosheit
Falschheit
Besorgtheit
Dürftigkeit
Wildheit
Unzivilisiertheit
Unbarmherzigkeit
Dummheit
Zurückgebliebenheit

Dunkelheit
Verschlossenheit
Schmierigkeit
Listigkeit
Achtlosigkeit
Gefräßigkeit
Selbstherrlichkeit
...heit ...keit ...

Postkarte: 5. Januar 1943

Eine *post kaart* schwarzweiß
Mit einem Bild des *Paradeplaats*.
Düster.
In der Mitte die Steinsäule des wütenden
Löwen.
Undeutlich vernehmbar schielt *JP Coen*
Hinter dem Hof des *Wit Huis* hervor.

Unten eine Briefmarke für 10 Cent.
Eine Mahnung zu einem
Postsparguthaben
Mit dem Gesicht eines Nippon-Soldaten
Dort ist geschrieben:

Aan M'n lieve moeder
Gelukkig Nieuw Jaar!

Das ist vielleicht das letzte
Denn Hermes der *Harmoni*
Wurden seine Füße gefesselt

Die Augen sind geschlossen
Die Flügel lösten sich

Daag!

Van je zoon
Hans E Van den Broecke.
Noordwijk – Pav 12 B
Batavia – Djakarta.

Einzug in die Stadt 1949

Wie von einem Augenzeugen erzählt

Seit gestern
Haben wir es bereits vorbereitet.
Blumen, Fahnen und Schultertücher
Für die jungen Kämpfer
Von Kerawang und Tanggerang.

Im Konvoi sind vielleicht noch
Jono, Idrus, Suratman und Bachtiar.
Unsere Kameraden, Freunde und Nachbarn
Die jetzt langhaarig, schmutzig und abgerissen sind.
Dabei waren sie früher ordentlich und adrett
gekleidet.
Alles wurde zu Zeiten von Nica verpfändet.

Seit gestern
Haben wir es bereits vorbereitet.
Gesänge und Medaillen
Die nicht angeheftet werden konnten
Und die nicht zu Gehör gebracht werden konnten
Alles umsonst,

Denn sie verschwanden eilends jagen
Nach Unterhaltung, Frauen, Beute und Wohnungen.
In den Gegenden Menteng, Matraman und Tanah
Abang.

Wir jubelten nur als wir in Kramat waren.
Suchten Gesichter die man nicht länger erkennen
konnte.
Wie ein fortgeschwemmtes Täschchen
Kehrte die Gruppe schweigend heim.
Dabei trugen sie eine welke Blume in der Hand
Zum Wegwerfen!

Herr Hendrik und sein Sohn si Jopie

Herr Hendrik ein echter Holländer hatte einen
kraftvollen Gang
So kraftvoll wie die Silhouettengestalt auf seiner
Getränkeflasche.
Manchmal nahm er eine *BSA*
Baujahr fünfundfünfzig.

Si Jopie war sein einziges Kind.
Ergebnis eines Heiratsvertrags mit einer
sundanesischen Witwe.
Si Jopie wurde junger Abkömmling eines
Europäers
Der gern andere belästigte.

Zum Glück war Herr Hendrik nicht bei der Nica
gewesen
Also konnte er im Kampung Jawa wohnen.
Als die Zeiten normal waren, arbeitete Herr
Hendrik bei *Nirom*
Als Rentner tat er Dienst bei *Philips-Ralin*.

Si Jopie schloss die Oberschule *Van Lith – Gunung Sahari* ab.
Zum Glück konnte er noch *Holland Spreken*.
Er schaffte es nicht Apotheker bei *Rathkamp* zu werden.
Schließlich wurde er Broker bei Unilever.

Die mächtigen Anschnauzer des Herrn Hendrik und seines Sohns si Jopie
Bekamen die Nachbarn zum Frühstück serviert.
Im Gästezimmer hing ein großes Plakat:

Rotterdamsche Lloyd
Die nie abfuhr um sie mitzunehmen.

Herr Hendrik war freundlich, aber schnell gereizt.
Si Jopie war kühn-arrogant und machte oft Probleme.
Ihr Gehalt ging drauf bei Prostituierten
Aus Krawang, Kuningan und Indramayu
Die sich in *Kali Got* und *Gang Hauber* aufhielten.

Manchmal alle drei Monate einmal
Machte sich Herr Hendrik *naar boven* nach Cisarua auf

Zusammen mit einigen indonesisch-holländischen
Mischlingen aus Manado
Seinen Kumpeln beim Kartenspiel.
Solange er weg war, stahl si Jopie oft
Den *Motorfiets*-Schlüssel seines Vaters
Um Jakarta-*round-round*-Fahrten zu unternehmen.

Regen kommt – die Ziege läuft davon -
Holland ist besoffen – drei Tage
Man lässt Wayang aufführen – bis zum Morgen
Japan ist besoffen – Holland läuft davon.

Herr Hendrik und sein Sohn si Jopie
Haben die Kirchentreppe vergessen
Haben das Datum von Weihnachten vergessen
Und haben ihr *jaarig* vergessen.
Herr Hendrik und sein Sohn si Jopie
Sind die übrig gebliebenen Enkel der Kompeni-
Soldaten
Die dauernd Probleme hatten als man sie
zurückließ.
Herr Hendrik starb plötzlich
Sein Sohn si Jopie starb bei einem Verkehrsunfall.
Beide wurden weggeworfen wie Abfall
Im *Velbak*

Habib

1

Ahlan!
Heiseres schweres Husten
Im ganzen arabischen Kampung.
Ein hoher Zaun
Türen den ganzen Mittag über fest geschlossen.
Spähende Frauen
Erkennen die Gäste
Hinter den Fenstergittern hervor.
Runde Augen
Senken sich auf das Ziel.
Nasen wie Bergrücken
Saugen allen Todesstaub ein.
Die Bazillen von Betawi raspeln fleißig ihre Kehlen

2

Ahlan!
Aus der trockenen Pharynxhöhle
Des Gottesfreundes im Sarong
Der auf einem Rattanstuhl sitzt
Kommt der Dampf einer Tasse Ingwergetränk

Die in der Mitte eines achteckigen Marmortisches
steht.
Ein kleiner Rosenkranz rotiert beständig am linken
Finger
Die rechte Hand stützt den Kopf mit den weißen
Haaren
Ein Haufen von Wolken hängt darüber:

3

mit einundzwanzig Jahren
hat er zum letzten Mal ein Wüstenwadi gesehen.
Von *Aden* nach Betawi
Nachdem er sich auf dem Deck eines englischen
Schiffes erbrach
Wurden seine Augen hellgrün.
Die Erde die er betrat war locker und fruchtbar.
Darin pflanzte er Hadithe und Rechtslehren ein
Die in jeder Zelle seines Gehirns wurzelten.

4

Herr wohin willste Herr
Will nach Pekojan.
Herr was willste verkaufen Herr
Will blutrote Korallen verkaufen.

Der Gottesfreund brachte Aloë-Extrakt ins
Kampung Bandan
Brachte das Buch in die Schule.
Verbreitete Duft im Haus und in der Koranschule.
Alle zehn Jahre einmal zog er seinen Burnus aus
Es ging nach Mekka um eine Steinsäule mit
Kieseln zu bewerfen ...
Seit 46 Jahren
Verbreitete sich der ausgesäte Samen
In den entlegenen Winkeln Betawis.
Und Habib möchte so gern nach Hause zurück!

5

Im ganzen arabischen Kampung.
Hüsteln und Näseln der Esel lösen einander ab.
Sie können sich nicht vor den Gläubigern
verstecken.
Und die Bazillen von Betawi jagen weiter,
Nagen ihre Kehlen und Lungen an.

Ba`da Ashar,
Nach dem Nachmittagsgebet.
Man beginnt die Türen zu öffnen
Ein Teil der Araber ruht sich in ihren
Unterkünften aus.

Sitzt auf Ruhebänken
Und saugt an der Wasserpfeife.

Ahlan ... Bib!
Sein Ingwergetränk ist schon kalt.
Zur Zeit der Trommel zum Abendgebet
Bewegen sich seine Finger nicht mehr.
Der Rosenkranz fällt herab
Seine Hand hängt schlaff herab
Berührt den Boden

Der kein Sand ist ...

Batavia Centrum

1933:
Einige chinesische Männer und Frauen
Hasten dahin Tragstangen auf den Schultern
Mit Körben rackern sich ab.
Gehen die engen Gassen
Der Ladengegend *Pintoe Ketjil* entlang.

1942:
Japan kam
Bagero, sagten sie
zu den Indochinesen mit ihrer Baumwollkleidung
die Mitleid erregten als ihre Lager
geräumt wurden.
Dieses Jahr ohne *Sin Chia*
Wird *Pia*-Kuchen nur mit Kokosnussabfall gefüllt.

1954:
Einige Amoys und Akews
Öffnen den Türriegel
Und warten auf Kleingeld
Um ihre aschgrauen Börsen zu füllen.

1963:
Ein Teil der hochgestellten Damen und Herren
Klemmt Steinchen unter die Tür.
Und lässt den Rauch von chinesischem Weihrauch
Ins Haus dringen.
Insgeheim zählen sie
Mit dem Abakus die Unglückstage.

1979:
Das Götterbild in der Küche ist neidisch
Wenn es sieht dass der Gott des Glücksspiels
Jeden Tag Weihrauchduft bekommt.
Marga Tan und Lie binden sich an *chiefen*
Ein Teil sucht den chinesischen Tempel auf
Der Rest sitzt ehrerbietig Mutter Maria gegenüber.

1992:
Einige ältere Damen und und Herren
Gehen wankend einander an der Hand haltend
Zur Veranda für *Tai-Chi*-Gymnastik.
Ihre Enkel schlafen inzwischen
Noch fest und tief in Singapur.

1998:
Die zerrissenen Eisernen Vorhänge knacken.

Zugleich damit fallen
Die magischen Steine *Dewi Kwam Im* und *Macan Pa Kua* herab
Verstreut zusammen mit der Asche ihrer Vorfahren.

2004
Eiserne Gitterkreuze schließen ihre Ghettos
In ganz Jakarta ab.
Sie wollen als Gast hin? Melden Sie sich vorher beim Wachdienst an.

Gasse der Zeit: Der Bahnhof Tanjung Priok

Die Nachmittagssonne streckt dem Zugangsweg
Geradewegs die Zunge entgegen und bricht durch
die Scheiben
Des *Art-Déco*-Gebäudes so hoch wie 50 Fuß

Sechsundzwanzig stählerne Stützpfeiler
Bilden in einem Halbkreis einen Bogen
Sie berühren einander ganz oben
Und bilden ein riesiges Maul
Dazu bereit jeden Menschen und auch Zug zu
schlucken.

Das dicke Gebäude hat zwei Kinder.
Die Arme krallen sich fest in die Erde.
Marmor oben – unten.
Die Innenwand geschmückt mit einem kleinen
Relief italienisch-javanischen Stils.
Von außen:
Das Gebäude sieht aus wie die Gestalt eines
urtümlichen Tiers.

Und nur die Zeit
Kann es zu Schutt und Asche machen.

Im Wartesaal:
Junge Mädchen schwatzen
Affektiert wie eine Familie von Spitzmäusen um
Brot streitet.
Die jungen *Menneer* tragen *Getsby*-Anzug und Mütze.
Sie haben die Arme in die Hüften gestemmt.
Sie warten auf die Waggons.
Manchmal spielen sie mit den langstöckigen
Schirmen.
Ähneln den Helden eines Stummfilms.

Einige Opas sitzen mit überkreuzten Beinen da.
Ernst lesen sie die Zeitung *Java Bode*.
Im Wartesaal für die VIPs plaudern einige Omas
miteinander.
Über die Aufführung von *Tonniel Miss Riboet*
Deren Plakat noch dort hängt.

Die jungen Matrosen sind gerade aus Singapur
gekommen.
Manchmal ruft sie die Schiffssirene am Pier.
Ambonesische Knil-Angehörige haben gerade

verloop ihrer Pflichten in Aceh
Sie stehen allein da
Und drehen sich Zigaretten mit dem aromatischen
Tabak der Marke: *Van Nelle.*

Der Bahnhofsvorsteher geht erhobenen Kopfes aus
seinem Wachhäuschen.
Stellt seine Sackuhr und plaudert einen Moment
mit dem Bahnsteigangestellten.
Dem Gleis gegenüber
Hocken Kulis und warten auf Befehle.
Eine ruhige Stimmung
Wie beim Warten auf die Ankunft eines
Leichnams.

Plötzlich
Werden alle erschreckt durch eine Gruppe junger
Abkömmlinge von Europäern
Von *Zandvoort* die scherzend hereinkommen.
Sie tragen Strandhüte und khakifarbene kurze
Hosen.
Ihr Schweiß riecht wie verdorbene Kokosmilch.

Ah...!
Ich glaube in vergangenen Zeiten zu sein,

Dem Bahnhof von Tanjung Priok in die Falle
gegangen.
Die Nachmittagssonne brennt gnadenloser.
Ihre Augen starren weit geöffnet auf das riesige
Maul
Das dringend seine Kiefer fest schließen möchte.
Denn die Stahlgerippe haben es sichtlich schon satt
Die Last der Zeit zu stützen.
Ihr Händedruck der schon Blasen bekommen hat
löst sich beinahe.
Von außen:
Ein Gebäude wie ein vernachlässigter *Dinosaurus*.
Und nur die Zeit
Kann es zu Schutt und Asche machen.

Im Wartesaal:
Angehörige der Eisenbahn-Jugendorganisation
trainieren Volleyball.
Ihre Stimmen hallen wider – Zeichen von
Fröhlichkeit.
Im ehemaligen VIP-Raum:
Männer spielen Badminton.
Die Räume wurden wie ein Termitenhaufen
In Büros und Lager abgeteilt.
Im Hof:

Menschen einer verwunschenen Welt liegen
ausgestreckt auf dem Boden.
Genau wie Flüchtlinge zur Zeit von Krieg und
Revolution.
In jeder Ecke:
Stinkender Abfall verbreitet sich.
Ein Geruch wie in einer Halle wo man früher
Schlachttiere verkaufte.

Zu der Zeit in der wir in seinem Bauch sind:
Es drängt sich uns die Frage auf,
Ist da noch mehr was er schlucken kann?
Der Bahnhof von Tanjung Priok
Ist ein riesiger Kokon der seinen eigenen Tod
Verfaulen lässt.

Seggelum Urbis Bataviae: 30 Mei 1619

Tuak nira
Arak Cina
Menggelitik tenggorokan
Dan memanaskan urat darah
Para pesinggah
Di pelabuhan *Sunda Calapa*.

Sisa uap getir asam cuka
Menerpa wajah Mayor singa
Dari kota Hoorn.
Seperti singa lapar,
Ia mengendap
                Mengintai
                Menghitung
                Menjerat
Dan memangsa
Kurban dalam jemarinya yang lentik.

Tiap hari, sesenti demi sesenti
Sehasta demi sehasta
Dengan rasa pasti

Sang Mayor jangkung
Menutup dan menyulap rawa *Jacatra*
Menjadi *Kastil Batavia.*

Seperti singa pemalu
Ia merayu para pesinggah, tentara, dan budak
Untuk merasakan runcing taringnya
Setajam tumbak.
Darah mereka menciprati
Tembok menara benteng *Mauritius* dan *Nassau.*
Sebagian yang mengental
Dikirim dan dipersembahkan oleh sang Mayor
Kepada leluhur orang-orang *Batavier*
Di Hollandia.

Amsterdam - Batavia

Buah cengkeh, pala dan lada
Sengat menyumbat hidung dan telinga
Para pelaut dan pedagang Walanda.
Angin kepulauan Maluku dan Banda
Mengabarkan timbunan rempah
Sampai ke lantai bawah tanah.

Amsterdam – Batavia sibuk menyiapkan
Palka, gudang, dan peta.
Awak di buritan mengendus membaui
Harum rempah
Dan laut memercikkan kilauan emas
Pada mata mereka.

Jangkar dilempar, meriam disulut
Bola-bola api bergema di Tidore,
Ternate, Banda, dan Ambone.
Mereka menjejal perut kapal
Dan mencabut pepohonan sampai ke akar
Rempah dilebur menjadi:
Tembok dan menara gereja

Penjara
Balai kota
Jalan raya
Istana
Dan *Club Concordia.*

Sebagian digadai untuk menjadi bekal:
Amunisi
Keju
Roti
Buku
Lampu
Brendy
Noni dan Nyai

Sisanya dibawa ke rumah surga
Yang di tiap pintu ditulis *Gloria.*
Di *Kebon Jahe, Kober*
Kapten Jas menunggu
Hermes, Mars, Apollo, Cupido, malaikat kecil, *Maria*,
Dan *Kristos*
Menyambut dan menemani tidur mereka setiap hari.

Sambil menunggu anak dan cucu mereka kembali
Dari Batavia.

Di Amsterdam
Para oma merenda dan berceloteh
Para opa mengisap pipa dan minum teh
Sementara di beberapa rumah minum pinggir pantai
Para nakhoda pemabuk menangisi kawan mereka
Yang tercekik dalam lumpur becek
Batavia.

Valckenier: 1740

Seperti Nero,
Ia duduk di veranda
Sambil memainkan lyra
Dan membiarkan lidah api
Menari di perkampungan orang Cina.

Mitos Vreemde Oosterlingen dan Inlander

Entreeprijzen Pasar Gambir: 1925

Op Gewone Dagen	*Volwassenen*	*Kinderen*
Europeanen	*f. 0.50*	*f. 0.25*
Vreemde Oosterlingen	*f. 0.25*	*f. 0.15*
Inlander f. 0.15	*f. 0.10*	

Timur adalah Timur
Yang jauh dan berbeda dari Barat
Yang selalu dibatasi oleh
Tembok:

Kecurigaan
Kedengkian
Kecurangan
Kekhawatiran
Kemelaratan
Keganasan
Kebiadaban
Kebrutalan
Kebodohan
Ketertinggalan

Kegelapan
Ketertutupan
Kejorokan
Keculasan
Ketidakpedulian
Kerakusan
Kelaliman
Ke…

Post Kaart: 5 Januari 1943

Sebuah *post kaart* hitam putih
Bergambar *Paradeplaats*.
Muram.
Di tengah tugu singa
Geram.
Samar-samar *JP Coen* menghardik
Dari balik halaman *Wit Huis.*

Di bawah perangko 10 Cent.
Peringatan tercapainya
Oeang taboengan pos.
Dengan wajah tentara Nippon
Tertulis:

Aan M`n lieve moeder
Gelukkig Nieuw Jaar!
Ini mungkin terakhir
Sebab Hermes di Harmonie
Kakinya sudah dirantai
Matanya ditutup

Sayapnya dilepas
Daag!

Van je zoon
Hans E Van den Broecke.
Noordwijk – Pav 12 B
Batavia – Djakarta.

Masuk Kota 1949

Seperti dikisahkan oleh seorang saksi mata

Sudah kami persiapkan
Sejak kemarin.
Kembang, bendera, dan selendang
Untuk pemuda pejuang
Dari Kerawang dan Tanggerang.

Dalam konvoi mungkin masih ada
Jono, Idrus, Suratman, dan Bachtiar.
Saudara, teman, dan tetangga kita
Yang kini menjadi gondrong, dekil, dan lusuh.
Padahal dahulu mereka necis dan parlente.
Semua sudah tergadai, saat Nica hadir.

Sudah kami persiapkan
Sejak kemarin.
Nyanyian dan lencana
Yang tak sempat tersematkan
Dan tak sempat didengarkan
Percuma,

Sebab mereka keburu menghilang memburu
Hiburan, perempuan, harta rampasan, dan
perumahan.
Di kawasan Menteng, Matraman, dan Tanah
Abang.

Kami hanya bersorak sesaat di Kramat.
Mencari wajah yang tak lagi dapat dikenali.
Seperti gedebong hanyut,
Rombongan terdiam pulang.
Sambil menenteng kembang layu
Untuk dibuang!

Tuan Hendrik dan Anaknya si Jopie

Tuan Hendrik Belanda totok berjalan tegap.
Setegap tokoh siluet pada botol minumannya.
Terkadang ia naik *BSA*
Buatan tahun lima puluh lima.

Si Jopie anak tunggalnya.
Hasil dari kawin kontrak dengan janda Sunda.
Si Jopie menjadi sinyo muda
Tukang goda.

Untung tuan Hendrik bukan Nica
Jadi bisa tinggal di Kampung Jawa.
Jaman normal, Tuan Hendrik bekerja di *Nirom*
Setelah pensiun bertugas di *Philips-Ralin*.

Si Jopie lulusan SMA *Van Lith - Gunung Sahari*.
Untung dia masih bisa *Holland Spreken*.
gagal jadi apoteker di *Rathkamp*
Akhirnya jadi broker di Unilever.

Sentak sengor suara Tuan Hendrik dan anaknya si
Jopie
Menjadi sarapan pagi para tetangga.
Di ruang tamunya dipajang poster besar:
Rotterdamsche Lloyd
Yang tak pernah berangkat mengangkut mereka.

Tuan Hendrik ramah, tapi suka senewen.
Si Jopie angkuh gagah dan suka bikin masalah.
Gaji mereka habis dieret para perempuan sundel
Dari Krawang, Kuningan, dan Indramayu
Yang mangkal di *Kali Got* dan *Gang Hauber.*

Terkadang tiga bulan sekali
Tuan Hendrik *naar boven* ke Cisarua
Bersama beberapa Indo-Menado
Konco main kartunya.
Selagi pergi – si Jopie suka mencuri
Kunci *Motorfiets* bapaknya
Untuk dipakai *round-round* Jakarta.

Hujan dateng – kambing lari
Blande mabok - tige hari
Wayang ditanggep – sampe pagi
Jepang mabok – Blande lari.

Tuan Hendrik dan anaknya si Jopie
Sudah lupa tangga gereja
Sudah lupa tanggal natal
Dan sudah lupa *jaarig* mereka.
Tuan Hendrik dan anaknya si Jopie
Adalah sisa cucu laskar kompeni
Yang terlunta di tinggal pergi.
Tuan Hendrik mati mendadak
Anaknya si Jopie mati ketabrak.
Keduanya dibuang seperti sampah
Ke *Velbak*

Habib

1

Ahlan!
Serak berat bebatukan
Sepanjang kampung Arab.
Pagar tinggi
Pintu mengatup sepanjang siang.
Para wanita mengintip
Memastikan tamu
Dari balik jeruji jendela.
Mata-mata bulat
Menukik pada sasaran.
Hidung-hidung seperti lengkung gunung
Mengisap semua debu kematian.
Para baksil Betawi rajin memarut tenggorokan
mereka

2

Ahlan!
Dari goa faring kering
Sang Habib sarungan
Duduk di kursi rotan
Secangkir gahwe jahe mengepul

Di tengah meja marmer segi delapan.
Tasbih kecil terus berotasi di jari kiri
Tangan kanan menyangga kepalanya yang
beruban
Segumpalan awan menggantung di atasnya:

3

sejak umur 21 tahun
Terakhir melihat wadi gurun.
Dari *Aden* menuju Betawi
Setelah muntah di dek kapal Inggris.
Matanya menghijau royo.
Tanah yang dipijak gembur-subur
Baik ditanam hadis dan fikih
Yang mengakar di setiap sel otaknya.

4

Wan mau kemane wan?
mau ke Pekojan.
Wan mau jual ape wan?
Mau jual merjan.

Sang habib membawa jadam menuju *Kampung*
Bandan
Membawa kitab menuju maktab

Menebarkan wewangian di rumah dan di
madrasah.
Sepuluh tahun sekali menanggalkan jubah
Menuju Makah melempar jumrah…
Selama 46 tahun
Benih yang ditanam
Menyebar di pelosok Betawi.
Dan Habib rindu kepingin pulang!

5

Sepanjang kampung Arab.
Dehem dan sengau keledai bersautan.
Mereka tak dapat sembunyi dari para penagih
Dan baksil Betawi terus mengejar,
Menggerogoti tenggorokan serta paru-paru
mereka.

Ba`da Ashar,
Pintu-pintu mulai terbuka
Sebagian Arab di pangkalan istirahat.
Duduk di bale-bale
sambil mengisap hoge.

Ahlan… Bib!
Gahwenya sudah dingin.

Saat beduk Maghrib,
Gerakan jarinya berhenti
Tasbihnya jatuh
Tangannya terkulai
Menyentuh lantai
Yang tak berpasir…

Batavia Centrum

1933:
Beberapa Encek dan Encim
Tergopoh-gopoh memikul
Keranjang keringat.
Menyusuri lorong sempit
Pertokoan *Pintoe Ketjil.*

1942:
Jeppun datang
Bagero, katanya
Kepada babah berbaju blacu
Yang memelas saat gudangnya
Dikuras.
Tahun ini tanpa *Sin Chia*
Kue Pia hanya berisi ampas kelapa.

1954:
Beberapa Amoy dan Akew
membuka grendel pintu
Dan menunggu recehan
Untuk mengisi pundi-pundi abu mereka.

1963:

Sebagian Enci dan Engkoh
Mengganjal pintu.
Dan membiarkan asap hio
Masuk ke rumahnya.
Diam-diam mereka menghitung
Hari-hari sial dengan sipoanya.

1979:

Taipekong dapur iri
Melihat dewa judi
Diberi dupa wangi setiap hari.
Marga Tan dan Lie mengikat *chiefen*
Sebagian *sampkai* ke vihara
Sisanya bersimpuh di hadapan Bunda Maria

1992:

Beberapa Encim dan Empe
tertatih bergandengan
Menuju emperan untuk senam *Tai-Chi*.
Sementara cucu mereka
Masih tertidur pulas di Singapura.

1998:

Tirai-tirai besi koyak berderak.
Bersamaan dengan itu
Batu giok *Dewi Kwam Im* dan *Macan Pa Kua*
Jatuh berserakan bersama abu leluhur mereka.

2004

Palang-palang besi menutupi ghetto-gheto mereka
Di seantero Jakarta.
Mau bertamu? Lapor dulu pada petugas jaga.

1998-2005

Lorong Waktu: Stasiun Kereta Api Tanjung Priok

Matahari sore lurus menjulurkan lidahnya
Pada lintasan dan memecahkan kaca-kaca
Gedung *Art-Deco* setinggi lima puluh kaki.

Dua puluh enam tiang baja penyangga
Melengkung setengah lingkaran
Mereka saling berjabatan di titik puncak
Dan membentuk mulut raksasa
Yang siap menelan setiap manusia juga kereta.

Gedung gemuk beranak dua.
Lengannya mencengkram kuat ke tanah.
Marmer atas – bawah.
Dinding dalam dihias relief kecil model Italy-Jawa.
Dari luar:
Gedung terlihat seperti sosok hewan purba.
Dan hanya waktu
Yang dapat menjadikannya puing abu.

Di dalam ruang tunggu:
Noni-noni bergaya

Bercakap seperti keluarga cecurut memperebutkan
roti.
Para *Menneer* muda mengenakan jas *Getsby* dan topi.
Berkacak pinggang.
Menunggu gerbong datang.
Sesekali memainkan payung bertongkat panjang.
Mirip tokoh film gagu.

Beberapa Opa duduk silang kaki.
Serius membaca koran *Java Bode*.
Di ruang tunggu VIP beberapa Oma
bercengkrama.
Tentang pertunjukan *Tonniel Miss Riboet*
Yang posternya masih terpampang di situ.

Para Matros muda baru tiba dari Singapura.
Sesekali serine kapal di dermaga memanggil mereka.
Knil Ambon baru *verloop* tugas di Aceh
Berdiri sendiri
Sambil melinting tembakau wangi merek: *Van Nelle*.

Kepala stasiun keluar dari pos jaga sambil
mendongak.
Mencocokan jam rante dan sesaat bercakap
dengan petugas peron.

Di seberang rel,
Para kuli berjongkok menunggu perintah.
Suasana tenang
Seperti menunggu kedatangan jenazah.

Tiba-tiba,
Semua dikejutkan oleh serombongan sinyo muda
Dari *Zandvoort* yang masuk sambil bercanda.
Mengenakan topi pantai dan celana pendek khaki.
Bau keringat mereka seperti santen basi.

Ah…!
Kukira berada di jaman baheula,
Ternyata terperosok di stasiun kereta api Tanjung
        Priok.
Matahari sore bertambah garang.
Matanya melotot menatap mulut raksasa
Yang ingin sekali mengatupkan rahang.
Sebab, rangka baja sudah terlihat bosan
Menyangga beban jaman.
Jabatan tangan mereka pun melepuh hampir terlepas.
Dari luar:
Gedung seperti *Dinosaurus* tak terurus.
Dan hanya waktu
Yang dapat menjadikannya puing abu.

Di dalam ruang tunggu:
Warga muda PJKA latihan Volley.
Suara mereka bergema - tanda gembira.
Di bekas ruang VIP:
Bapak-bapak main Badminton.
Ruang-ruang disekat seperti sarang rayap
Untuk kantor dan gudang.
Di pelataran:
Orang antah berantah bergelimpangan.
Persis seperti pengungsi jaman perang revolusi.
Di tiap pojok:
Ampas pesing menyebar.
Baunya seperti bekas tempat penjualan hewan
kurban.

Saat berada di dalam perutnya:
Kita menjadi bertanya,
Masih adakah yang dapat ditelannya lagi?
Stasiun kereta api Tanjung Priok
Adalah kepompong raksasa yang membusuki
Kematiannya sendiri.

The Translators

Debbie Cole

Debbie Cole lived in Jakarta between the ages of four and twelve. She earned her Ph.D in linguistics and linguistic anthropology at the University of Arizona in 2004. Her dissertation, "Performing 'unity in diversity' in Indonesian poetry: Voice, ideology, grammar, and change", examined public poetry performances in Indonesian in Yogyakarta and Central Java during the *Reformasi* period. In 2007, she received a Senior Fulbright Scholar award for research and lectureship, and served as a visiting professor in the Master's Program in Culture and Media Studies at Gadjah Mada University. She is currently an associate professor of linguistics at the University of Texas–Rio Grande Valley. She is a co-editor of the forthcoming *Lontar Anthology of Indonesian Poetry*.

Michael Groß

Michael Groß went to university in Munich and Berlin (MA in 1984, PhD in 1987). From 1988 to 1992 he worked as a lecturer of the German Academic Exchange Service (DAAD) in linguistics and German language at the University of Indonesia in Jakarta. Following his return to Germany, he worked as a teacher of German as a foreign language. He also began to work as a translator of various kinds of Indonesian texts. Since 2004 he has served as co-editor of *Kita*, a journal published by the German-Indonesian Society (Deutsch-Indonesische Gesellschaft), three times a year.

INDONESIA

NUSA TENGGARA TIMUR

The province of East Nusa Tenggara, made up of more than 500 islands, has a population of about 5 million. But the region's most famous inhabitant is The Komodo Dragon; the largest living species of lizard in the world. The colorful textiles of this province often feature an abstract depiction of this primeval beast.

PACIFIC OCEAN